JIM COWART AND MATTHEW HARTSFIELD
JENNIFER COWART AND JORGE ACEVEDO

GROUNDED *in* PRAYER

PARTICIPANT AND LEADER BOOK

A COMMUNITY GROUP RESOURCE

This book is printed on acid-free paper.

ISBN: 978-1-5018-4904-6

Unless otherwise noted, all scripture quotations are from the Common English Bible. Copyright © 2011 by the Common English Bible. All rights reserved. Used by permission. www.CommonEnglishBible.com.

The Lord's Prayer found throughout is taken from the Book of Common Prayer. *The Book of Common Prayer and Administration of the Sacraments and other Rites and Ceremonies of the Church According to the Use of the Protestant Episcopal Church in the United States of America Together with The Psalter or Psalms of David* (New York: James Pott and Co., 1892).

Other Community Group Resources for Small Groups:

Grab, Gather, Grow: Multiply Community Groups in Your Church
Grab, Gather, Grow: Video
Living the Five: Participant and Leader Book
Living the Five: Video
Hand Me Downs Participant and Leader Book: Leaving a Legacy
Hand Me Downs: Video
Grounded in Creed Participant and Leader Guide
Grounded in Creed: Video

17 18 19 20 21 22 23 24 25 26—10 9 8 7 6 5 4 3 2 1
MANUFACTURED IN THE UNITED STATES OF AMERICA

Contents

Sessions

Appendices

Community Group Leaders

Welcome

Greetings from Jim and Matthew.

Jesus's original followers wanted to know how to talk to God. They desired a more powerful prayer life. Jesus taught them The Lord's Prayer as a model for how to pray. For centuries Christ-followers have prayed The Lord's Prayer with sincere faith. After two thousand years, The Lord's Prayer still inspires our souls and serves as a great pattern for how to communicate effectively with God.

Welcome to *Grounded in Prayer*. We invite you to join us, and our friends Jorge and Jennifer, as we go on a journey that will build your faith and help you pray with greater joy and purpose. We will discuss The Lord's Prayer line-by-line. You'll also hear questions and insights from several of our friends who gathered with us to learn more about this powerful prayer and how it can change your life.

During this six-week study you'll have opportunities to share your own ideas and experiences with your group. You'll discuss scripture that supports The Lord's Prayer, and learn from each other while building rich relationships in your group.

We're excited about what God is about to do in your life and in your group over these next six weeks. We have prayed fervently to God that you will experience a vital next step in your faith through this study.

Using This Workbook

1   The table of contents includes three sections: (1) Sessions, (2) Appendices, and (3) Community Group Leaders. Familiarize yourself with the appendices. Some of them will be used in the sessions themselves.

2   If you are facilitating/leading or coleading a small group, the Community Group Leaders section offers tested experience from others that will encourage and help you avoid many common obstacles to effective community-group leadership.

3   Use this workbook as a guide, not as a straitjacket. If the group responds to the lesson in an unexpected but honest way, go with that. If you think of a better question than the next one in the lesson, ask it. Take to heart the insights included in the Frequent Questions pages and the Community Group Leaders section.

4   Enjoy your community-group experience.

5   Pray before each session—for your group members, for your time together, and for wisdom and insights.

6   Read the Outline of Each Session on the next pages so that you understand how the sessions will flow.

Outline of Each Session

A typical group session will include the following sections.

WEEKLY MEMORY VERSE. Each session opens with a memory verse that emphasizes an important truth from the session. This is an optional exercise, but we believe that memorizing scripture can be a vital part of aligning our minds with God's will. We encourage you to give this important habit a try. The verses for our six sessions are also listed in the appendices.

BEFORE GROUP. Each lesson opens with a brief thought to help you prepare for the session. Think about the particular subject you will explore with your group. Make it a practice to read these thoughts before the session.

DURING GROUP. The foundation for spiritual growth is an intimate connection with God and God's family. You build that connection by sharing your experience with a few people who really know you and who have earned your trust. This is helpful preparation for sharing what Christ has done in your life with anyone you meet—which is what a disciple is ready to do. This section includes some simple questions to get you talking. Share as much or as little of your story as you prefer. Each session typically offers two options. Get to know your whole group by using the icebreaker question(s) or by conversation with your spiritual partner(s) for encouragement in your spiritual journey.

HEAR GOD'S STORY. In this section, you'll read the Bible and begin to see how God's story aligns with yours. You'll have an opportunity to read a passage of scripture and discuss the teaching and the text. You won't focus on accumulating information but on how you should live in light of God's word. Apply the insights from scripture practically and creatively, from your heart as well as your head. At the end of the day your desire is to allow God's word to transform your life.

STUDY NOTES. This brief section provides additional commentary, background, or insights on the passage you'll study in the Hear God's Story section.

APPLICATION. God wants you to be a part of his kingdom—to weave your story into his. That will bring change. It will require you to go God's way rather than your own. This won't happen overnight, but it should happen steadily. By making small, simple choices, we can change our direction. The Bible advises to "be doers of the word and not only hearers" (James 1:22 CEB). Many people skip over this aspect of the Christian life because it's challenging, awkward, or simply too much work for their busy schedules. But Jesus wanted all disciples to know him personally, carry out God's commands, and help outsiders connect with him. This doesn't necessarily mean preaching on street corners. It could mean welcoming newcomers, hosting a short-term group in your home, or walking through this study with a friend. In this study, you'll have an opportunity to go beyond Bible study to biblical living.

AFTER GROUP. If you have time and want to dig deeper into more Bible passages about the topic at hand, we've provided additional passages and questions. Your group may choose to read and prepare ahead of each meeting to cover more biblical material. If you prefer not to do study homework, this section will provide you with plenty to discuss within the group. These options allow individuals or the whole group to expand their study while still accommodating those who can't do homework or are new to your group.

DAILY DEVOTIONS. Each week on the Daily Devotions pages, we provide scriptures to read and reflect on between sessions—a month's worth of reflections to keep God's word near your heart. This provides you with a chance to slow down, read just a small portion of scripture each day, and reflect and pray through it. You'll then have a chance to respond in your notes to what you've read. Use this section to seek God on your own throughout the week. This time at home should begin and end with prayer. Don't be in a hurry; take enough time to hear God's direction.

01

Our Father

Lord my God, how fantastic you are!
You are clothed in glory and grandeur!

PSALM 104:1 CEB

THE LORD'S PRAYER

Our Father, who art in heaven,
hallowed be thy Name,
thy kingdom come,
thy will be done,
on earth as it is in heaven.
Give us this day our daily bread.
And forgive us our trespasses, as we forgive those who trespass against us.
And lead us not into temptation, but deliver us from evil.
For thine is the kingdom, and the power, and the glory, forever and ever. Amen.

Before Group

Help People Share

Each of us has a story. The events of our life—good, bad, wonderful, or challenging—have shaped who we are. God knows your story and intends to redeem it—to use every struggle and every joy to ultimately bring you to God. When we share our stories with others, we give them the opportunity to see God at work.

When we share our stories, we also realize we are not alone—that we have common experiences and thoughts and that others can understand what we are going through. Your story can encourage someone else, and telling it can lead to a path of freedom for you and for those you share it with.

If your group is new, welcome newcomers. Introduce everyone—you may even want to have name tags for your first meeting.

During Group

1. Prayer

Open your group with prayer. This should be a brief, simple prayer in which you invite God to give you insight as you study. You can pray for specific requests at the end of the meeting or stop momentarily to pray if a particular situation comes up during your discussion.

2. Roster

As you begin this first meeting, get contact information for every participant. Take time to pass around a copy of the Community Group Roster (found on page 66), a sheet of paper, or one participant can pass his or her study guide, opened to the Coummunity Group Roster. Ask someone to make copies or type up a list with everyone's information and e-mail it to the group during the week.

3. Community Group Agreement

Whether your group is new or ongoing, it's always important to reflect on and review your values together. On page 57 is a Community Group Covenant with the values we've found most useful in sustaining healthy, balanced groups. We recommend that you choose one or two values—ones you haven't previously focused on or have room to grow in—to emphasize during this study. Choose ones that will take your group to the next stage of intimacy and spiritual health.

4. Community Group Calendar

We recommend you rotate host homes on a regular basis, and let the hosts lead the meeting. Healthy groups rotate leadership. This helps to develop every participant's ability to shepherd a few people in a safe environment. Even Jesus gave others the opportunity to serve alongside him (Mark 6:30-44). Look at the Frequent Questions in the appendices for additional information about hosting or leading the group.

The Community Group Calendar on page 58 is a tool for planning who will host and lead each meeting. Take a few minutes to determine hosts and leaders for your remaining meetings. Don't skip this important step! It will revolutionize your group.

5. Segments of Life

Take a look at the segments diagram on the next page and write the names of two or three people you know who need to know Christ. Commit to praying for God's guidance and an opportunity to share with each of them. Perhaps they would be open to joining the group? Share your lists with the group so you can all be praying for the people you've identified.

6. Opening Questions

Begin your time together by using the following questions and activities to get people talking.

> What brought you here? What do you hope to get out of this group?

> Are you familiar with The Lord's Prayer? What's your experience with it?

7. DVD

Have a volunteer read the following before you watch the DVD:

The average American speaks between 13,000 and 20,000 words a day. From the moment we say "Where's the coffee?" in the morning to our last "Good night" before bed, we spend our lives talking to other people.

Yet some of us find it more difficult to talk to God. New believers and lifelong Christians sometimes struggle with how to pray and what to say when we do. But we were created to be in relationship with God, and just as our relationships with friends and family require communication, prayer is absolutely vital to knowing God better and growing in our faith.

Fortunately, during his time on earth Jesus gave us a model prayer that can help us connect with God. Over the next six weeks, we'll learn not only what The Lord's Prayer can teach us about prayer but what it can teach us about the God who loves us and longs to hear from us.

FAMILY (immediate or extended)	
FAMILIAR (neighbors, kids' sports teams, school, and so forth)	
FRIENDS	
FUN (gym, hobbies, hangouts)	
FIRM (work)	

Watch the DVD

Use the notes space provided on page 67 to record key thoughts, questions, and things you want to remember or follow up on. After watching the video, have someone read the discussion questions and direct the discussion among the group. As you go through each of the subsequent sections, ask someone else to read the questions and direct the discussion.

Video Discussion Questions

How comfortable are you talking to God in your own words? Is this normal for you or do you prefer more structured or written prayers?

How does this model prayer provide "jumping off points" for other prayers?

Is it easy or difficult to refer to God as your father? Why?

Why does praising God pave the way for gratitude?

You should start by saying the God of the universe and the creator of all is your Dad. This is how Jesus talked to God, and with this prayer he's inviting us to draw near to him.

Hear God's Story

Read 1 John 3:1-2.

¹See what kind of love the Father has given to us in that we should be called God's children, and that is what we are! Because the world didn't recognize him, it doesn't recognize us.

²Dear friends, now we are God's children, and it hasn't yet appeared what we will be. We know that when he appears we will be like him because we'll see him as he is. (CEB)

What are some of the privileges that come with being a child of earthly parents? What are some of the privileges we receive as God's children?

How does the world's understanding of God affect its understanding of us as God's church?

What are we going to be in the future? (v. 2)

Study Notes

The Lord's Prayer is shared in the Gospels of Matthew and Luke. Later in the New Testament, Paul explores more of what it means for God to be our Father. In Galatians 4, Paul writes,

But when the fulfillment of the time came, God sent his Son, born through a woman, and born under the Law. This was so he could redeem those under the Law so that we could be adopted. Because you are sons and daughters, God sent the Spirit of his Son into our hearts, crying, "Abba, Father!" Therefore, you are no longer a slave but a son or daughter, and if you are his child, then you are also an heir through God. (Gal 4:4-7 CEB)

Abba means dad. It is what a human child would call a human father as a term of endearment, and this passage is saying that all of us who follow Jesus become God's adopted sons and daughters —and he becomes our dad. God loves us like the best father loves his child and has changed us from a slave to sin to an "heir" of God's love.

Application

What should I do with this?
In this section, talk about how you will apply the wisdom you've learned from the teaching and Bible study. Then think about practical steps you can take in the coming week to live out what you've learned.

How can we apply this lesson as a group?
Examples:

How can we apply this lesson as individuals?
Examples:

Our Father

Prayer

Ask, "How can we pray for you this week?" Invite everyone to share, but don't force the issue.
Be sure to write prayer requests in your Prayer Requests and Praise Reports section on page 61.

Close your meeting with prayer.

After Group

For additional study:
If you feel God nudging you to go deeper, take some time before the next meeting to dig into God's word. Explore the Bible passages related to this session's theme on your own, and jot your reflections in a journal or in this guide. A great way to gain insight on a passage is to read it in several different translations. You may want to use a Bible app or website to compare translations.

Read Galatians 3:26-29.

What does it mean to "clothe" yourself with Christ?

How does our shared identity as God's children remove divisions like race and class?

Read Genesis 12:1-3.

How are we part of this promise to Abraham?

Read Luke 19:37-40.

Why were the disciples praising Jesus?

How does this passage illustrate what it means to worship and honor God?

What does Jesus mean in verse 40?

Daily Devotions

This week how will you interact with the Bible? Can you commit to spending time in daily prayer or study of God's word? Use the Daily Devotions section to guide you. Tell the group how you plan to follow Jesus this week, and then, at your next meeting, talk about your progress and challenges.

Day 1

Read 1 Corinthians 8:6.

For us believers,
There is one God the Father.
All things come from him, and we belong to him.
And there is one Lord Jesus Christ.
All things exist through him, and we live through him. (CEB)

Reflect:

What does it mean to live for God our Father? What does it mean to live through Christ?

Day 2

Read Psalm 68:5.

Father of orphans and defender of widows
is God in his holy habitation. (CEB)

Reflect:

God is not a reluctant father or a distant father—he is a loving, compassionate Father who protects and cares for each of his children. Thank God for loving you like a caring dad!

Day 3

Read Isaiah 64:8.

But now, LORD, you are our father.
We are the clay, and you are our potter.
All of us are the work of your hand. (CEB)

Reflect:

In this poetic, beautiful verse, the prophet notes that not only does God love us as children but as creation. What does it mean for God to form you and shape your life?

Day 4

Read John 4:24.

God is spirit, and it is necessary to worship God in spirit and truth. (CEB)

Reflect:

When we worship in the Spirit, we worship as children of God (see the Study Notes for more on this). When we worship in truth, we acknowledge who God is and what he has done. How can you grow in your worship of God?

Day 5

Read John 1:12.

But those who did welcome him,
those who believed in his name,
he authorized to become God's children. (CEB)

Reflect:

We had no control over our first birth or our human parents, but we get to make a choice about becoming children of God. If you are not yet a follower of God, consider what you have learned this week. Are you ready to accept Christ and become a child of God?

Day 6

Use the following space to write any thoughts God has put in your heart and mind about the things we have looked at in this session and during your Daily Devotions time this week.

02

God's Kingdom

I have come down from heaven not to do my will, but the will of him who sent me.

JOHN 6:38 CEB

THE LORD'S PRAYER

Our Father, who art in heaven,
hallowed be thy Name,
thy kingdom come,
thy will be done,
on earth as it is in heaven.
Give us this day our daily bread.
And forgive us our trespasses, as we forgive those who trespass against us.
And lead us not into temptation, but deliver us from evil.
For thine is the kingdom, and the power, and the glory, forever and ever. Amen.

Before Group

Help People Share

As we said last week, when we share our stories with others, we give them the opportunity to see God at work. Your story is being shaped, even in this moment, by being part of this group. In fact, few things can shape us more than community.

When we share our stories, we can encourage someone else and learn. We experience the presence of God as God helps us be brave enough to reveal our thoughts and feelings.

God's Kingdom

During Group

1. Prayer

Open your group with prayer. This should be a brief, simple prayer in which you invite God to be with you as you meet. You can pray for specific requests at the end of the meeting or stop momentarily to pray if a particular situation comes up during your discussion.

2. Opening Questions

Use the following to get people talking.

What do you tend to pray about most often?

Share one thing you learned from your devotions this past week.

3. Segments of Life

In the last session we asked you to write some names in the segment diagram. Who did you identify as the people in your life who need to meet Jesus? Go back to the diagram on page 8 to help you think of various people you come in contact with on a regular basis—people who need to know Jesus more deeply. Consider ideas for action, and make a plan to follow through on one of the ideas this week.

4. Spiritual Partners

Pair up with someone in your group. This person will be your spiritual partner for the rest of this study. He or she doesn't have to be your best friend. Instead, this person will simply encourage you to complete the goals you set for yourself during this study. Following through on a resolution is tough when you're on your own; it makes all the difference to have a partner to cheer you on. Spend a few minutes introducing yourselves, if you don't already know each other, and share one insight you had from last week's session or from your Daily Devotions this past week.

5. DVD

Have a volunteer read the following before you watch the DVD:

The Lord's Prayer is a pattern for our own prayers, so it's significant to consider what Jesus includes in it—and what he doesn't. So often our prayers focus on what we want—the promotion, the bigger paycheck, the healthy family, the resolution of problems. But that's not how Jesus teaches us to pray. Instead, he asks for what God wants: for God's spiritual kingdom to become more real here on earth, for God's purposes to prevail, and for us to be obedient to God's will.

Praying this way requires trusting that God knows best and that God's will is better than ours. It requires humility because asking God to reign over our lives means acknowledging we need to grow and change. And it requires a shift in perspective from our individual "kingdoms" and concerns to God's heart for the entire world. This is more difficult than presenting God with a list of things we want, but it's the next step in learning to pray like Jesus—and part of growing to be more like him.

Watch the DVD

Use the notes space provided on page 67 to record key thoughts, questions, and things you want to remember or follow up on. After watching the video, have someone read the discussion questions and direct the discussion among the group. As you go through each of the subsequent sections, ask someone else to read the questions and direct the discussion.

Video Discussion Questions

What does Jesus mean when he refers to God's "kingdom"?

Is it difficult for you to ask for God's plan and will instead of your own? How does praying this way change you?

How is God's will done in heaven? What are some ways we can do God's will here on earth?

Why does it take courage to pray this way?

> We get to make choices, and Jesus is teaching us that part of prayer is submitting our own will to his.

Hear God's Story

Read Matthew 13:31-33, 44-46.

31 He told another parable to them: "The kingdom of heaven is like a mustard seed that someone took and planted in his field. 32 It's the smallest of all seeds. But when it's grown, it's the largest of all vegetable plants. It becomes a tree so that the birds in the sky come and nest in its branches."

33 He told them another parable: "The kingdom of heaven is like yeast, which a woman took and hid in a bushel of wheat flour until the yeast had worked its way through all the dough. . . .

44 "The kingdom of heaven is like a treasure that somebody hid in a field, which someone else found and covered up. Full of joy, the finder sold everything and bought that field.

45 "Again, the kingdom of heaven is like a merchant in search of fine pearls. 46 When he found one very precious pearl, he went and sold all that he owned and bought it." (CEB)

In Matthew, God's kingdom is called "the kingdom of heaven." How is God's kingdom like a mustard seed? In what ways does the kingdom grow?

How is God's kingdom like yeast? In what ways does it spread and gain influence?

How is God's kingdom a hidden treasure? What should our response be when we find the kingdom?

How is God's kingdom like a pearl? What would it look like for you to respond to the kingdom like the merchant?

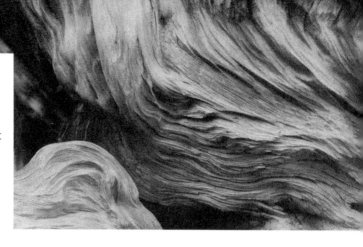

Study Notes

When we pray for God's kingdom to come on earth, we're living in both the "now" and the "not yet." In one sense the kingdom arrived when Jesus came to earth. It's intended as a spiritual reality now for all who follow him. But in another sense the kingdom is yet to come because all that God has for us and everything God intends the kingdom to be won't be fully realized until Jesus returns. This means the present matters to God because even now God is building the kingdom among God's people. But it also means we have a great future to look forward to because when God's kingdom comes once and for all, in perfection and for eternity, it will be like nothing we can imagine.

So we can look forward to "kingdom come" when we get to experience a wonderful forever with our King. But we can also pray that God's will would be done here on earth as Jesus invites us to know more of God. When we pray this way we receive blessings on earth *and* in heaven.

Application

In this section, talk about how you will apply the wisdom you've learned from the teaching and Bible study. Then think about practical steps you can take in the coming week to live out what you've learned.

How can we apply this lesson as a group?
    Examples:

How can we apply this lesson as individuals?
    Examples:

God's Kingdom

Prayer

Ask, "How can we pray for you this week?" Invite everyone to share, but don't force the issue. Be sure to write prayer requests in your Prayer Requests and Praise Reports section on page 61.

Close your meeting with prayer.

After Group

For additional study:

If you feel God nudging you to go deeper, take some time before the next meeting to dig into God's word. Explore the Bible passages related to this session's theme on your own, and jot your reflections in a journal or in this guide. A great way to gain insight on a passage is to read it in several different translations. You may want to use a Bible app or website to compare translations.

Read Matthew 26:36-39.

Why did Jesus bring his disciples with him to the garden?

Reread verse 38. How do Jesus's emotions at this point make his obedience to God's will even more amazing?

When have you ever had to face a trial or a challenge that you've asked God to take away? When has God ever asked you to do something really difficult?

Read Luke 17:20-21.

How do the Pharisees' question reveal their misunderstanding of the kingdom?

Why can't the coming of the kingdom be observed with our senses?

What does it mean that the kingdom is in our midst?

Daily Devotions

This week how will you interact with the Bible? Can you commit to spending time in daily prayer or study of God's word? Use the Daily Devotions section to guide you. Tell the group how you plan to follow Jesus this week, and then, at your next meeting, talk about your progress and challenges.

Day 1
Read Matthew 7:21.

"Not everybody who says to me, 'Lord, Lord,' will get into the kingdom of heaven. Only those who do the will of my Father who is in heaven will enter." (CEB)

Reflect:
It is good to acknowledge Jesus with our words, but it's even better to follow him with our actions. Ask God to help you do God's will!

Day 2
Read Daniel 2:44.

But in the days of those kings, the God of heaven will raise up an everlasting kingdom that will be indestructible. Its rule will never pass to another people. It will shatter other kingdoms. It will put an end to all of them. It will stand firm forever. (CEB)

Reflect:
In ancient times, kingdoms and land were constantly changing as kings rose and fell in power. But God's kingdom will never fail, never change hands, and never be conquered.

Day 3
Read Psalm 143:8.

Show me the way I should go,
*   because I offer my life up to you. (CEB)*

Reflect:
Jesus taught his disciples to pray for God's will to be done because he knew this was a prayer God would answer! God wants to guide you and give you wisdom as you seek to follow him. Be bold in praying for his guidance.

Day 4
Read Luke 6:46.

"Why do you call me 'Lord, Lord' and don't do what I say?" (CEB)

Reflect:
If you're serious about following Jesus as king of your life, it means submitting to the rule of God's kingdom. Ask God to help you understand his will and his ways.

Day 5
Read Romans 12:2.

Don't be conformed to the patterns of this world, but be transformed by the renewing of your minds so that you can figure out what God's will is—what is good and pleasing and mature. (CEB)

Reflect:
When we spend time with God in prayer, he transforms us and actually makes us able to understand his will. The more you pray like Jesus, the more you will become like Jesus.

Day 6
Use the following space to write any thoughts God puts in your heart and mind about the things we have looked at in this session and during your Daily Devotions time this week.

Daily Needs

My God will meet your every need out of his riches in the glory
that is found in Christ Jesus.

PHILIPPIANS 4:19 CEB

THE LORD'S PRAYER

Our Father, who art in heaven,
hallowed be thy Name,
thy kingdom come,
thy will be done,
on earth as it is in heaven.
Give us this day our daily bread.
And forgive us our trespasses, as we forgive those who trespass against us.
And lead us not into temptation, but deliver us from evil.
For thine is the kingdom, and the power, and the glory, forever and ever. Amen.

Before Group

Help People Share

Each of us has a story. The events of our life—good, bad, wonderful, or challenging—have shaped who we are. God knows your story, and God intends to redeem it—to use every struggle and every joy to ultimately bring you to God. When we share our stories with others, we give others the opportunity to see God at work.

When we share our stories, we also realize we are not alone—that we have common experiences and thoughts and that others can understand what we are going through. Your story can encourage someone else, and telling it can lead to a path of freedom for you and for those you share it with. Be an example of good listening. The goal is not to just learn information but to develop deeper friendships.

During Group

1. Prayer

Open your group time with prayer. This should be a brief, simple prayer, in which you invite God to give you insight as you study. You can pray for specific requests at the end of the meeting or stop momentarily to pray if a particular situation comes up during your discussion.

2. Opening Questions

Use the following to get people talking.

> When have you had to trust God for the basics of life: food, shelter, clothing?

> Share one thing you learned from your devotions this past week.

3. Spiritual Partners

Sit with your spiritual partner. If your partner is absent or you are new to the group, join with another pair or someone who doesn't yet have a partner. If you haven't established your spiritual partnership yet, do it now. Take a few minutes to talk about your goals for the remaining three weeks of this study. How do you sense God moving in your life, and how do you want to respond? Share these goals with each other and spend a few minutes praying together. See page 59 in the appendices for a resource that can help you.

4. DVD

Have a volunteer read the following before you watch the DVD:

These days, carbs is a bad word. Some of us are trying to slim down by eating fewer processed foods, so we're cutting things like bread and sweets from our diets. Others skip the carbs because they need to avoid gluten. Whatever the reason, it's hard to open a magazine about fitness or visit a website about health without hearing that carbs are the enemy.

But in this study, we see Jesus praying for bread! Of course, this prayer has nothing to do with high-protein diets or eating gluten-free; instead, it's an invitation for us to tell God about the needs in our lives and ask for divine provision and care. As we've learned, God is a Father who loves us, so Jesus is telling us God cares about our lives. We've also learned about God's great power and authority, so God is more than able to provide for us when we trust. Whether you've sworn off carbs forever or you eat pasta with every meal, today's lesson reminds us that God will take care of us—no matter what we need.

Watch the DVD

Use the notes space provided on page 67 to record key thoughts, questions, and things you want to remember or follow up on. After watching the video, have someone read the discussion questions and direct the discussion among the group. As you go through each of the subsequent sections, ask someone else to read the questions and direct the discussion.

Video Discussion Questions

Matthew made the point that our "daily bread" is a way of saying our daily needs. What are some of your needs that only God can meet?

How might God want to use you to answer this prayer for someone else?

How is it difficult for you to be patient in waiting for answers to prayer?

How does praying this prayer change us?

We're saying we need God even more than we need food. We need the Provider more than the provision.

Hear God's Story

Read John 6:25-35.

[25] When they found him on the other side of the lake, they asked him, "Rabbi, when did you get here?"
[26] Jesus replied, "I assure you that you are looking for me not because you saw miraculous signs but because you ate all the food you wanted. [27] Don't work for the food that doesn't last but for the food that endures for eternal life, which the Human One will give you. God the Father has confirmed him as his agent to give life."
[28] They asked, "What must we do in order to accomplish what God requires?"
[29] Jesus replied, "This is what God requires, that you believe in him whom God sent."
[30] They asked, "What miraculous sign will you do, that we can see and believe you? What will you do? [31] Our ancestors ate manna in the wilderness, just as it is written, He gave them bread from heaven to eat."
[32] Jesus told them, "I assure you, it wasn't Moses who gave the bread from heaven to you, but my Father gives you the true bread from heaven. [33] The bread of God is the one who comes down from heaven and gives life to the world."
[34] They said, "Sir, give us this bread all the time!"
[35] Jesus replied, "I am the bread of life. Whoever comes to me will never go hungry, and whoever believes in me will never be thirsty." (CEB)

This dialogue happened shortly after Jesus fed thousands of people with bread and fish. How does that context enhance your understanding of this passage?

Why do the people following Jesus ask him for a sign? (vv. 30-31)

What is the "true bread" that God gives us?

Obviously we get physically hungry and thirsty even though we follow Christ. What does Jesus mean in verse 35?

Study Notes

As the team shared on the video this week, "daily bread" can be taken literally—as our food for the day—or metaphorically to represent the consistent needs all of us experience. Either way, the point of this line of the prayer is that God wants to meet these needs and God welcomes our prayers for them.

But think about the passage we just studied; Jesus probably used the word *bread* in this prayer on purpose. As Matthew taught, the Israelites received manna each morning for forty years as they wandered in the wilderness. This was literally daily bread—crispy, slightly sweet bread that God provided so the people could eat as they journeyed toward the promised land. And as we read in John 6, Jesus calls himself the bread of life—the true nourishment that can fill our whole being and give us spiritual life.

Jesus also might have been thinking about his encounter with Satan at the beginning of his ministry. In Luke 4 we read about Satan tempting Jesus. It says,

Jesus returned from the Jordan River full of the Holy Spirit, and was led by the Spirit into the wilderness. There he was tempted for forty days by the devil. He ate nothing during those days and afterward Jesus was starving. The devil said to him, "Since you are God's Son, command this stone to become a loaf of bread."
Jesus replied, "It's written, People won't live only by bread." (Luke 4:1-4 CEB)

In this example, we see Jesus seeking God's will and glory, as we talked about last week, and Jesus shows us by his example that we can trust God to provide the "bread" we need.

So as simple as this part of The Lord's Prayer seems on the surface, it is pointing to deeper insights about who God is and how to trust God. We can certainly pray for daily physical food, and we should also be praying for the daily spiritual "food" that Jesus can provide. God wants to give us both!

Application

In this section, talk about how you will apply the wisdom you've learned from the teaching and Bible study. Then think about practical steps you can take in the coming week to live out what you've learned.

How can we apply this lesson as a group?
    Examples:

How can we apply this lesson as individuals?
    Examples:

Prayer

Ask, "How can we pray for you this week?" Invite everyone to share, but don't force the issue.
Be sure to write prayer requests in your Prayer Reqests and Praise Reports section on page 61.

Close your meeting with prayer.

After Group

For additional study:
Take some time between now and our next meeting to dig into God's word. Explore the Bible passages related to this session's theme. Jot down your reflections in a journal or in this guide. You may even want to use a Bible website or app to look up commentary on these passages. If you like, share what you learn with the group the next time you meet.

Read Matthew 6:25-34.

Why does Jesus point to birds and flowers when he encourages us not to worry?

Why is it reassuring to remember that God knows about your needs? (v. 32)

What does it mean to seek God's kingdom first?

Read 2 Corinthians 9:10-11.

How is God described in these verses? What does this tell you about God's character?

What does it mean to be enriched? What are the areas of life where you need God's enrichment?

How does generosity with God's gifts lead to thanksgiving?

Daily Devotions

This week how will you interact with the Bible? Can you commit to spending time in daily prayer or study of God's word? Use the Daily Devotions section to guide you. Tell the group how you plan to follow Jesus this week, and then, at your next meeting, talk about your progress and challenges.

Day 1

Read Psalm 107:8-9.

Let them thank the LORD for his faithful love
and his wondrous works for all people,
because God satisfied the one who was
parched with thirst,
and he filled up the hungry with good things!
(CEB)

Reflect:

Remembering God's faithful love and deeds can remind us that God is enough. If you are thirsty or hungry for anything today, believe that God will satisfy you.

Day 2

Read Philippians 4:19.

My God will meet your every need out of his riches in the glory that is found in Christ Jesus. (CEB)

Reflect:

Jesus owns everything, created everything, rules everything. He can certainly meet your needs today!

Day 3

Read Isaiah 58:11.

The LORD will guide you continually
and provide for you, even in parched places.
He will rescue your bones.
You will be like a watered garden,
like a spring of water that won't run dry. (CEB)

Reflect:

God promises that if we obey, God will never fail us. Are there areas of life where you don't think you have "enough"? Are you obeying God in those areas?

Day 4

Read 2 Corinthians 9:8.

God has the power to provide you with more than enough of every kind of grace. That way, you will have everything you need always and in everything to provide more than enough for every kind of good work. (CEB)

Reflect:

God will never ask you to do something without equipping you for it. Thank God today for the ways your life is blessed, and pray about how God's gifts should equip you to serve.

Day 5

Read Philippians 4:6.

Don't be anxious about anything; rather, bring up all of your requests to God in your prayers and petitions, along with giving thanks. (CEB)

Reflect:

The part of The Lord's Prayer that we studied this week is a pattern for how to follow the instruction in this passage. Take a few minutes today to take your needs to God, and be thankful for God's faithfulness to you.

Day 6

Use the following space to write any thoughts God puts in your heart and mind about the things we looked at in this session and during your Daily Devotion time this week.

04

Forgiveness

Because as high as heaven is above the earth,
that's how large God's faithful love is for those who honor him.
As far as east is from west—
that's how far God has removed our sin from us.

PSALM 103:11-12 CEB

THE LORD'S PRAYER

Our Father, who art in heaven,
hallowed be thy Name,
thy kingdom come,
thy will be done,
on earth as it is in heaven.
Give us this day our daily bread.
And forgive us our trespasses, as we forgive those who trespass against us.
And lead us not into temptation, but deliver us from evil.
For thine is the kingdom, and the power, and the glory, forever and ever. Amen.

Before Group

Help People Share

As we said in previous lessons, sharing our personal stories builds deeper connections among group members. Your story may be exactly what another person needs to hear, and listening to others' stories is an act of love and kindness to them—and could very well help them to grow in faithfulness.

During Group

1. Prayer

Open your group with prayer. This should be a brief, simple prayer, in which you invite God to give you insight as you study. You can pray for specific requests at the end of the meeting or stop momentarily to pray if a particular situation comes up during your discussion.

2. Opening Questions

Use the following to get people talking.

Who in your life are you struggling to forgive?

Share one thing you learned from your devotions this past week.

3. Spiritual Partners

Sit with your spiritual partner. If your partner is absent or if you are new to the group, join with another pair or someone who doesn't yet have a partner. If you haven't established your spiritual partnership yet, do it now.

Share one prayer request and one thing you want to thank God for. Spend some time praying about what you've shared.

4. DVD

Have a volunteer read the following before you watch the DVD:

Theologian Lewis Smedes is well known for his observation that "when we forgive, we set a prisoner free and then discover that the prisoner we set free was us."* In his book Boundaries, *Henry Cloud writes, "Forgiveness gives me boundaries because it unhooks me from the hurtful person, and then I can act responsibly, wisely. If I am not forgiving them, I am still in a destructive relationship with them."† Other authors and scientists have noted that forgiving others can lead to lower blood pressure and lower levels of depression and anxiety, while holding on to our hurts and our anger can harm us both physically and psychologically.*

These are all sufficient reasons for people to learn how to forgive. But as Christians we have a more important reason—because God first forgave us. By sending Jesus to die for us and take the penalty of sin on our behalf, God made a way to forgive us of every wrong for all time—and to reconcile with us in a relationship of love and grace. God forgave us our trespasses, our debts, and our sins, and today we're going to talk about how God can help us extend the same kind of forgiveness to others. This may give us greater freedom, more peace of mind, and better health. It will definitely make us more like our Savior.

* Lewis B. Smedes, *Forgive and Forget: Healing the Hurts We Don't Deserve* (1984; repr., New York: HarperSanFrancisco, 1996), x.

† Henry Cloud and John Townsend, *Boundaries: When to Say Yes, How to Say No to Take Control of Your Life* (Grand Rapids: Zondervan, 1992), 269.

Watch the DVD

Use the notes space provided on page 67 to record key thoughts, questions, and things you want to remember or follow up on. After watching the video, have someone read the discussion questions and direct the discussion among the group. As you go through each of the subsequent sections, ask someone else to read the questions and direct the discussion.

Video Discussion Questions

How is forgiveness of others a form of releasing them—and releasing ourselves?

How does God's forgiveness of you help you forgive others?

React to Jen's statement that the only thing a marriage can't survive is unforgiveness. Why is it so essential that spouses (as well as parents, children, and close friends) learn to forgive each other? Why is resentment so poisonous?

Why is "forgive and forget" an unreasonable expectation? What does it mean to forgive and remember in a new way?

We are sinful people ourselves and we find it hard to forgive others. God is perfect and holy and yet willing to forgive.

Hear God's Story

Read Ephesians 1:7-10.

7 We have been ransomed through his Son's blood, and we have forgiveness for our failures based on his overflowing grace, 8 which he poured over us with wisdom and understanding. 9 God revealed his hidden design to us, which is according to his goodwill and the plan that he intended to accomplish through his Son. 10 This is what God planned for the climax of all times: to bring all things together in Christ, the things in heaven along with the things on earth. (CEB)

In this passage, God is described as rich in grace, which God "poured over" us. How does this perspective on God's forgiveness affect you?

What is the mystery of God's will that is revealed to us?

How is God's will fulfilled in Christ?

How does our forgiveness through Jesus's sacrifice bring us unity with God?

Study Notes

On the video, the team reminded us that when we can't imagine forgiving what someone has done to us, we should compare it to what we have done to God. This is not to minimize our own pain or hurt, which may be very real, but it is a way to put that suffering into perspective.

The night before Jesus died, he prayed, "My Father, if it's possible, take this cup of suffering from me. However—not what I want but what you want" (Matt 26:39 CEB). In the culture of that day, talking about a "cup" was a way of describing what one had experienced or was going to experience. For instance, in Psalm 23:5 David says "my cup is so full it spills over," which means that his life has been abundantly blessed.

So when Jesus prays this desperate prayer in Matthew 26, he is asking God to take the experience of suffering away from him. In fact, some theologians have suggested that far greater than any physical pain that Jesus experienced on the cross was the spiritual and emotional anguish he endured. While he was on the cross, he bore the weight of every sin, of every person, of every day of human history. Everything you would ever do, big and small, and everything that person you're struggling to forgive has ever done, and every other sin of the world was put on him.

The injustices that have been done to you and the pain you have felt are real, but if you are struggling to forgive the things you've experienced, spend some time reflecting on what Jesus experienced on your behalf. Ask for his strength to forgive others as he has forgiven you.

Application

In this section, talk about how you will apply the wisdom you've learned from the teaching and Bible study. Then think about practical steps you can take in the coming week to live out what you've learned.

How can we apply this lesson as a group?
    Examples:

How can we apply this lesson as individuals?
    Examples:

Prayer

Ask, "How can we pray for you this week?" Invite everyone to share, but don't force the issue. Be sure to write prayer requests in your Prayer Requests and Praise Reports section on page 61.

Close your meeting with prayer.

After Group

For additional study:
If you feel God nudging you to go deeper, take some time before the next meeting to dig into the word. Explore the Bible passages related to this session's theme on your own and jot your reflections in a journal or in this guide. A great way to gain insight on a passage is to read it in several different translations. You may want to use a Bible app or website to compare translations.

Read Colossians 3:12-14.

What is our motivation for following the recommendations in these verses? (v. 12)

What does it mean to "be tolerant with each other" (CEB)?

How does love bring unity?

Read Luke 17:3-5.

What is the condition for forgiveness that Jesus gives?

What must happen if the condition is met?

What is the significance of the apostles' reaction—saying "Increase our faith!"? Why would that be their response to this teaching?

Daily Devotions

This week how will you interact with the Bible? Can you commit to spending time in daily prayer or study of God's word? Use the Daily Devotions section to guide you. Tell the group how you plan to follow Jesus this week, and then, at your next meeting, talk about your progress and challenges.

Day 1

Read Ephesians 4:32.

Be kind, compassionate, and forgiving to each other, in the same way God forgave you in Christ. (CEB)

Reflect:

As Jim mentioned in this week's teaching, the Bible is full of passages urging us to forgive like God does. Who do you need to show more kindness, compassion, and forgiveness to this week?

Day 2

Read Matthew 5:43-45.

"You have heard that it was said, You must love your neighbor and hate your enemy. But I say to you, love your enemies and pray for those who harass you so that you will be acting as children of your Father who is in heaven." (CEB)

Reflect:

This is a challenging teaching! Is there an enemy in your life you need to pray for? Try praying just a short prayer for that person today. How did it make you feel?

Day 3

Read Mark 11:25.

And whenever you stand up to pray, if you have something against anyone, forgive so that your Father in heaven may forgive you your wrongdoings. (CEB)

Reflect:

We are commanded to forgive! What old hurts or resentments do you need to let go of in order to move forward?

Day 4

Read 1 John 1:9.

If we confess our sins, he is faithful and just to forgive us our sins and cleanse us from everything we've done wrong. (CEB)

Reflect:

Why is it so important that we tell God about our sins? What do you need to confess to God today?

Day 5

Read Psalm 69:5.

God, you know my foolishness;
*   my wrongdoings aren't hidden from you. (CEB)*

Reflect:

We end this week with a final reminder that God already knows all of our mistakes. Our guilt is known; let's confess it and find forgiveness and freedom.

Day 6

Use the following space to write any thoughts God has put in your heart and mind about the things we have looked at in this session and during your Daily Devotions time this week.

05

Temptation

The one who is in you is greater than the one who is in the world.

1 JOHN 4:4 CEB

THE LORD'S PRAYER

Our Father, who art in heaven,
hallowed be thy Name,
thy kingdom come,
thy will be done,
on earth as it is in heaven.
Give us this day our daily bread.
And forgive us our trespasses, as we forgive those who trespass against us.
And lead us not into temptation, but deliver us from evil.
For thine is the kingdom, and the power, and the glory, forever and ever. Amen.

Before Group

Help People Share

Telling our personal stories builds deeper connections among group members. Sharing our stories requires us to be honest. We can help each other be honest and open by creating a safe place; be sure that your group is one where confidentiality is respected, where there is no such thing as "stupid questions," where you listen without criticizing each other.

During Group

1. Prayer

Open your group with prayer. This should be a brief, simple prayer, in which you invite God to give you insight as you study. You can pray for specific requests at the end of the meeting or stop momentarily to pray if a particular situation comes up during your discussion.

2. Opening Questions

Use the following to get people talking.

> What is one sin or temptation you struggle with on a regular basis? Do not feel compelled to share with the group unless you want to!

> Share one thing you learned from your devotions this past week.

3. Spiritual Partners

Sit with your spiritual partner. If your partner is absent or if you are new to the group, join with another pair or someone who doesn't yet have a partner. If you haven't established your spiritual partnership yet, do it now.

Answer this question: How has participating in this group affected your personal relationship with God?

4. DVD

Have a volunteer read the following before you watch the DVD:

Sometimes we joke about being tempted to eat too much or spend too much money. "I just can't even have cookies in the house!" we'll say, or "That shoe sale was calling my name—I had to buy something!"

We've all eaten a few too many desserts or bought something we don't need, but in the course of our lives we also face more serious temptations: to

skim a little money off the top because the boss won't know, to flirt with that stranger instead of going home to our spouse, to watch videos we shouldn't, to use our words to hurt others, to take the shortcut of a lie instead of doing the hard work of telling the truth.

We live in a fallen world ravaged by sin, so this week's passage from The Lord's Prayer addresses the reality of our need for God as both a protector and a deliverer. Evil surrounds us and the evil one lies in wait for us—but whether it's sweets or shoes or something far more serious, God will help us face our trials and fight our sin.

Watch the DVD

Use the notes space provided on page 67 to record key thoughts, questions, and things you want to remember or follow up on. After watching the video, have someone read the discussion questions and direct the discussion among the group. As you go through each of the subsequent sections, ask someone else to read the questions and direct the discussion.

Video Discussion Questions

What is the difference between God allowing us to experience trials and leading us into temptation?

Who do you have in your life you can share struggles with? Who do you have to keep you accountable?

What does it mean to be delivered from evil? Does this mean God will remove all struggles from our lives?

How did Jesus prove his victory over evil? What is our part in overcoming the evil still in the world?

Hear God's Story

Read 1 John 5:18-20.

18 We know that everyone born from God does not sin, but the ones born from God guard themselves, and the evil one cannot touch them. 19 We know we are from God, and the whole world lies in the power of the evil one. 20 We know that God's Son has come and has given us understanding to know the one who is true. We are in the one who is true by being in his Son, Jesus Christ. This is the true God and eternal life. (CEB)

Those of us who are Christians do continue to sin; what does verse 18 mean?

Who is the "one" who keeps us safe?

How does the evil one control the world? Why do you think God allows this right now?

Jesus has given us the ability to understand God's truth. What is our responsibility as a result?

Study Notes

One of the audience members shared today that she has a favorite verse of scripture that she says to herself during times of temptation. This is an excellent (and biblical) way for us to fight sin in our own lives.

Psalm 119:11 says, "I keep your word close, in my heart, so that I won't sin against you" (CEB). When we take the time to memorize scripture, we internalize it into our heads and our hearts, making it part of ourselves and the way we think.

Romans 12:2 says, "Don't be conformed to the patterns of this world, but be transformed by the renewing of your minds so that you can figure out what God's will is—what is good and pleasing and mature" (CEB). When we transform our minds with God's word, we are better able to hear wisdom and guidance during difficult situations.

Philippians 4:8 says, "From now on, brothers and sisters, if anything is excellent and if anything is admirable, focus your thoughts on these things: all that is true, all that is holy, all that is just, all that is pure, all that is lovely, and all that is worthy of praise" (CEB). When we focus on things that honor God and help us grow, there's less room in our minds and in our lives for things that lead to sin and pain.

Jesus demonstrated this for us at the beginning of his ministry. Three of the four Gospels record his time of temptation in the wilderness. Each time he was tempted to sin against God, he responded by quoting scripture—right to Satan's face! You can read about this in Matthew 4:1-11, Mark 1:9-13, or Luke 4:1-13. Take a few minutes this week to reflect on Jesus's approach to temptation and choose a verse that addresses one of your own struggles to begin memorizing and making part of your life.

Application

In this section, talk about how you will apply the wisdom you've learned from the teaching and Bible study. Then think about practical steps you can take in the coming week to live out what you've learned.

How can we apply this lesson as a group?
   Examples:

How can we apply this lesson as individuals?
   Examples:

Prayer

Ask, "How can we pray for you this week?" Invite everyone to share, but don't force the issue.
Be sure to write prayer requests in your Prayer Requests and Praise Reports section on page 61.

Close your meeting with prayer.

After Group

For additional study:

Take some time between now and our next meeting to dig into God's word. Explore the Bible passages related to this session's theme on your own. Jot down your reflections in a journal or in this guide. You may even want to use a Bible website or app to look up commentary on these passages. If you like, share what you learn with the group the next time you meet.

Read 1 Corinthians 10:13.

Why do you think Paul emphasizes that we all face the same kinds of temptations?

This verse says God won't let us be tempted unbearably. Why does God allow us to be tempted at all?

What are some examples of how God provides ways out of temptation?

Read 1 Peter 5:8-10.

What do we learn about the devil in verse 8?

What is part of our motivation for resisting the evil one? (v. 9)

What is the promise of this passage?

Daily Devotions

This week how will you interact with the Bible? Can you commit to spending time in daily prayer or study of God's word? Use the Daily Devotions section to guide you. Tell the group how you plan to follow Jesus this week, and then, at your next meeting, talk about your progress and challenges.

Day 1
Read 1 John 2:16-17.

Everything that is in the world—the craving for whatever the body feels, the craving for whatever the eyes see and the arrogant pride in one's possessions—is not of the Father but is of the world. And the world and its cravings are passing away, but the person who does the will of God remains forever. (CEB)

Reflect:
This verse reinforces the idea that sin and the temptations to sin do not ever come from God. How do the things of the world drag your eyes away from Christ?

Day 2
Read James 1:12.

Those who stand firm during testing are blessed. They are tried and true. They will receive the life God has promised to those who love him as their reward. (CEB)

Reflect:
Here is another passage with wonderful promises for those who resist sin and place their trust in God. Today, ask God to give you the perseverance and strength to endure the tests in your life.

Day 3
Read Ephesians 6:11.

Put on God's armor so that you can make a stand against the tricks of the devil. (CEB)

Reflect:
We are not powerless when it comes to the devil! Read Ephesians 6 to see all of the tools God has given us!

Day 4
Read James 1:13-14.

No one who is tested should say, "God is tempting me!" This is because God is not tempted by any form of evil, nor does he tempt anyone. Everyone is tempted by their own cravings; they are lured away and enticed by them. (CEB)

Reflect:
This verse makes it clear that God does not lead us to temptation—and that temptation is strong! It drags us, it entices us, but God can help us stand firmly!

Day 5
Read Hebrews 2:18.

He's able to help those who are being tempted, since he himself experienced suffering when he was tempted. (CEB)

Reflect:
As we talked about this week, Jesus knows what it is to face the devil and win. No matter what you are facing, know that he understands and he wants to help you.

Day 6
Use the following space to write any thoughts God has put in your heart and mind about the things we have looked at in this session and during your Daily Devotions time this week.

06

Power and Glory

God's kingdom isn't about words but about power.

1 CORINTHIANS 4:20 CEB

THE LORD'S PRAYER

Our Father, who art in heaven,
hallowed be thy Name,
thy kingdom come,
thy will be done,
on earth as it is in heaven.
Give us this day our daily bread.
And forgive us our trespasses, as we forgive those who trespass against us.
And lead us not into temptation, but deliver us from evil.
For thine is the kingdom, and the power, and the glory, forever and ever. Amen.

Before Group

Help People Share

As we have said in previous lessons, sharing our personal stories builds deeper connections among group members. Your story may be exactly what another person needs to hear to encourage or strengthen them. And listening to others' stories is an act of love and kindness to them—and could very well help them grow spiritually.

During Group

1. Prayer

Open your group with prayer. This should be a brief, simple prayer, in which you invite God to give you insight as you study. You can pray for specific requests at the end of the meeting or stop momentarily to pray if a particular situation comes up during your discussion.

2. Opening Questions

Use the following to get people talking.

What has surprised you most about this group?

Where did God meet you over the last six weeks?

3. Spiritual Partners

Take time in this final session to connect with your spiritual partner. What has God been showing you through these sessions? What positive changes has your partner noticed in you? Check in with each other about the progress you made in your spiritual growth during this study. Make plans about whether you will continue your relationship after the group has concluded.

4. DVD

Have a volunteer read the following before you watch the DVD:

The final lines of The Lord's Prayer are not found in the Bible and thus are words of praise added later. This is a fitting conclusion to everything that comes before—because God is our Father, because God is able to accomplish his will and bring his kingdom, because God can meet every need and forgive every sin, because God protects us from the evil one and rescues us from temptation, we can say with all of our hearts, "God, we give you all the power, and we know that all the glory belongs to you!"

As we close this series, we'll learn more about God's power and glory, and we'll think about all of it in light of our eternity with Christ.

Watch the DVD

Use the notes space provided on page 67 to record key thoughts, questions, and things you want to remember or follow up on. After watching the video, have someone read the discussion questions and direct the discussion among the group. As you go through each of the subsequent sections, ask someone else to read the questions and direct the discussion.

Video Discussion Questions

How does this prayer prompt us to close in worship with words about God's glory?

What aspects of the final line of the prayer make it bold, even radical?

Why does the Bible include so many reminders about God's power?

How does Jesus show us the glory of God?

> In heaven we will know and experience everything we're saying about God in this prayer, and we'll experience it for eternity.

Hear God's Story

Read Ephesians 1:18-23.

[18] I pray that the eyes of your heart may be enlightened in order that you may know the hope to which he has called you, the riches of his glorious inheritance in his holy people, [19] and his incomparably great power for us who believe. That power is the same as the mighty strength [20] he exerted when he raised Christ from the dead and seated him at his right hand in the heavenly realms, [21] far above all rule and authority, power and dominion, and every name that is invoked, not only in the present age but also in the one to come. [22] And God placed all things under his feet and appointed him to be head over everything for the church, [23] which is his body, the fullness of him who fills everything in every way. (CEB)

What is the hope we are called to?

How is Jesus superior to every authority and all other power?

How should it change us if we believe we have the same power living in us?

How does Jesus show his power through the church?

Study Notes

At the beginning of the video, the team talked about moving beyond memorization of this prayer and putting it into our own words—for instance, instead of saying, "hallowed be your name," you might say, "God, you're awesome!" This would be a great way to reflect on what you've learned over the last six weeks and cement the insights and ideas of the prayer into your heart. Here's the full text of the prayer. In a journal or in this guide, take some time to rewrite it in words that express the same ideas but in your own way. Then read through your finished prayer and pray it to God!

Our Father who art in heaven,
hallowed be thy Name,
thy kingdom come,
thy will be done,
on earth as it is in heaven.
Give us this day our daily bread.
And forgive us our trespasses, as we forgive those who trespass against us.
And lead us not into temptation, but deliver us from evil.
For thine is the kingdom, and the power, and the glory, forever and ever. Amen.

Application

In this section, talk about how you will apply the wisdom you've learned from the teaching and Bible study. Then think about practical steps you can take in the coming week to live out what you've learned.

How can we apply this lesson as a group?
    Examples:

How can we apply this lesson as individuals?
    Examples:

Prayer

Ask, "How can we pray for you this week?" Invite everyone to share, but don't force the issue. Be sure to write prayer requests in your Prayer Requests and Praise Reports section on page 61.

Close your meeting with prayer.

After Group

For additional study:

If you feel God nudging you to go deeper, take some time to dig into the word. Explore the Bible passages related to this session's theme on your own and jot your reflections in a journal or in this study guide. A great way to gain insight on a passage is to read it in several different translations. You may want to use a Bible app or website to compare translations.

Read Hebrews 1:1-4.

How is Jesus "the heir of everything"?

What aspects of Jesus's power are revealed in this passage?

How does Jesus radiate God's glory to us?

Read Philippians 2:6-11.

Jesus is the reflection of God's power and glory, yet he chose to humble himself and to serve. What does that tell us about how we are to live?

What does it mean to be "in the form of God"? What does it mean that Jesus took "the form of a slave"?

What power and authority did Jesus receive as a result?

Daily Devotions

Day 1

Read Psalm 19:1.

Heaven is declaring God's glory;
the sky is proclaiming his handiwork. (CEB)

Reflect:

How do the heavens and the skies tell us about God? What does the beauty of nature tell you about God's nature?

Day 2

Read 2 Timothy 1:7.

God didn't give us a spirit that is timid but one that is powerful, loving, and self-controlled. (CEB)

Reflect:

We share in God's power when we follow God and allow the Holy Spirit into our lives. How do you need God's power to help you grow in love and self-discipline?

Day 3

Read Romans 11:36.

All things are from him and through him and for him.
May the glory be to him forever. Amen. (CEB)

Reflect:

God gives us all things, oversees all things, and is glorified by everything in creation. Today, write out a prayer of thanksgiving for the ways God is working in your life.

Day 4

Read Ephesians 3:20-21.

Glory to God, who is able to do far beyond all that we could ask or imagine by his power at work within us; glory to him in the church and in Christ Jesus for all generations, forever and always. Amen. (CEB)

Reflect:

This is another doxology full of words proclaiming God's power. What an amazing thought that God can do even more than what we can dream of—and that God does it through divine power in our lives!

Day 5

Read 1 Corinthians 4:20.

God's kingdom isn't about words but about power. (CEB)

Reflect:

We put our trust in Christ because he backed up his words with actions—he rose from the dead! As we close this series, reflect on God's amazing power and ask God to work in a new way in your life.

Day 6

Use the following space to write any thoughts God puts in your heart and mind about the things we have looked at in this session and during your Daily Devotions time this week.

Appendices

Resources to make your small group experience even better!

Frequent Questions

What do we do at our first community group meeting?

Have a party! Make it fun. A "get to know you" coffee, meal, or dessert is a great way to launch a new study. You may want to review the Community Group Covenant (page 57), and discuss the names of a few friends you can invite to join your group. Don't jump right into study time. Get to know each other first. Even if you are already close, talk about something that happened that week.

Where do we find new participants for our community group?

Adding people to a group can be troubling. We get comfortable with each other, and then find it awkward to bring in another relationship. Even new groups of four or five people can sense this intimacy. And groups of friends who have been together will lose a few people but not think to recruit new participants. After your group prays about their purpose, create together a list of people to welcome from your neighborhood, your workplaces, your children's school, your families, the gym, and so on. Each participant would then invite the people on his or her list. Church leaders are also willing to announce that your community group is open and welcoming, or put the list of groups in a bulletin insert.

It's very healthy to remain open and welcoming so that new participants can join your group. Attrition happens in groups as people move to new locations, or take on new leadership roles, or hear the calling into other ministry opportunities. So before the group becomes small,

making it at risk of stopping, stay open—God will send interesting people your way. You might meet your best friend forever.

How long will community groups meet?

Most community groups meet weekly for at least their first five weeks. Every other week can work too. In the early months, try to meet weekly as a group. When life happens or when a job requires someone to miss a meeting, they won't miss a month if the group meets occasionally.

At the end of this community group study, each group member may choose whether to stay in the community group or look for another study. Some groups launch relationships that last many years, and others are temporary signposts on the journey into another group experience. The journey is what matters.

Can we do this study on our own?

One of the best ways to do this study is not with a full house but with a few friends, coworkers, or neighbors. You may prefer to gather with another couple to walk through this study. Then you can be flexible about other ways to grow deeper in friendship by going to see a movie or going out for dinner. God's spirit is present even when two or three are seeking guidance through the scriptures and in prayer (Matt 18:20).

What if this group is not working for us?

Sometimes a group encounters a personality conflict, life-stage difference, geographical distance, varied levels of spiritual maturity, or many other differences. Take a breath and pray for God's guidance. When this six-week study is complete, decide whether your group is a good fit for you. It often takes eight to nine weeks for a small group to bond and appreciate each other, so don't bail out before the six weeks of this study are up—God might have something to teach you. Also, don't run from conflict or prejudge a person or group before you have given them a chance. Have you ever noticed that as soon as a difficult person leaves a group, someone else in the group will take their place! God is still working in your life too!

Who is the leader?

Healthy community groups rotate hosts/leaders and homes on a regular basis. By sharing the leadership or hosting, participants can learn their unique gifts and feel satisfaction from their contribution. This study guide and the Holy Spirit can keep things on track even when you rotate discussion leaders. Christ promised to be in your midst when you gather. Ultimately, God is your leader each step of the way.

How do we handle the child care needs in our group?

Handle child care with sensitive thinking. Ask the group to openly suggest solutions. If one approach does not work, adjust to another. Many groups share the cost of a babysitter (or two), who can watch the kids in a different part of the house or yard. Another option is to use one home for the kids and a second home (close by or a phone call away) for the adults. Or if the group has enough adults, the responsibility can be rotated among the adults for the children, either in the same home or in another home nearby. Kids respond well when they see how other parents care for them. Of course, typically each parent can make their own arrangements for their children. Speak openly with each other about the responsibility and the resolution.

Community Group Covenant

OUR PURPOSE
To provide a predictable environment where participants experience authentic community and spiritual growth.

OUR GROUP EXPECTATIONS

- Showing Up
  We will make an effort through our presence in each group meeting. We will call or e-mail if we cannot attend or will arrive late. (If the Group Calendar is completed, participants will know when to meet.)

- Comfortable Environment
  Participants will be heard and feel loved. They will know this because we listen to each other's answers and judgments with respect. Our replies will be gentle and gracious because we are at different stages of spiritual maturity, and our "imperfections" indicate where we are each under construction, moving on toward a complete and whole life together.

- Keeping Secrets
  When participants share private and intimate aspects of their personal life, we will not share this outside the group, and we will avoid gossiping about others outside the group.

- Healthy Growth
  Participants will serve others with their God-given gifts, and we will help others in the group discover their own strengths and gifts.

- Everyone in Ministry
  Every participant will take on a role or responsibility over time in the group.

- Rotating Hosts and Homes
  Each participant is encouraged to host the group in his or her home and rotate the responsibility of facilitating a meeting. (See the Community Group Calendar on page 58.)

Community Group Calendar

Planning and calendaring can help ensure the greatest participation at every meeting. At the end of each meeting, review this calendar. Be sure to include a regular rotation of host homes and leaders, and encourage every member to take on some role of responsibility in the group.

DATE	LESSON	HOST HOME	HOSPITALITY	LEADER	ADMIN	PRAYER
5/4	1	Mike	Sandra	Billy	Lori	Sam
	1					
	2					
	3					
	4					
	5					
	6					

Team Roles:

Host Home:
Prepare your home to host the group meeting.

Hospitality:
Welcome people in the group and provide refreshments.

Leader:
Prepare for lesson and facilitate discussion during meeting.

Admin:
Send out e-mails, keep roster, and take notes to share.

Prayer:
Open/close in prayer and send out prayer requests.

Spiritual Partner Check-In

Briefly check in each week, and write down your personal plans and progress targets for the next week. This could be done before or after the meeting, on the phone, through an e-mail message, or even in person from time to time.

	OUR PLAN	OUR PROGRESS
My Name:		
Spiritual Partner's Name:		
Week 1		
Week 2		
Week 3		
Week 4		
Week 5		
Week 6		

Memory
Verses

SESSION ONE
Let my whole being bless the LORD!
    LORD my God, how fantastic you are!
    You are clothed in glory and grandeur!
Psalm 104:1 CEB

SESSION TWO
I have come down from heaven not to do my will, but the will of him who sent me.
John 6:38 CEB

SESSION THREE
My God will meet your every need out of his riches in the glory that is found in Christ Jesus.
Philippians 4:19 CEB

SESSION FOUR
Because as high as heaven is above the earth,
    that's how large God's faithful love is for those who honor him.
As far as east is from west—
    that's how far God has removed our sin from us.
Psalm 103:11-12 CEB

SESSION FIVE
The one who is in you is greater than the one who is in the world.
1 John 4:4 CEB

SESSION SIX
God's kingdom isn't about words but about power.
1 Corinthians 4:20 CEB

Prayer Requests
and Praise Reports

	Prayer Requests	Praise Reports	
Session 1			Session 1
Session 2			Session 2
Session 3			Session 3
Session 4			Session 4
Session 5			Session 5
Session 6			Session 6

Community Group Leaders

Key resources to help your leadership experience be the best it can be.

Starting a New Community Group

New community groups can often grow and multiply because the participants gather with more openness than existing small groups. An "open house" is a particularly good way to meet and break the ice with each other before the first session of a group study. The group can also discuss other persons to invite as the study begins. Discuss what each participant can expect from the group, and start off the right way by praying briefly for each other.

Don't worry about ending up with too many people; you can always have one discussion circle in the living room and another in the dining room after you watch the lesson.

In the Gospels, especially in Matthew and Luke, food around a table with teaching is often in the mix when the disciples and seekers are engaged in learning and growing spiritually. So when launching a new community group, tasty desserts or a basic meal will probably stimulate the joy of doing life together.

Ask the participants to introduce themselves and share how or why they are present in this group. If the participants seem shy, you can ask some leading questions:

- What is your most memorable experience from a vacation?
- What is one thing that you appreciate about your community, town, or city?
- Describe a couple things about your childhood that the participants would not know.

Review the Community Group Covenant and talk about each person's expectations and priorities.

Finally, place an empty seat or two in the middle of your group and encourage the group participants to think about a person who could fill that chair or seat over the next few weeks. Provide postcards and have each participant complete one or two invitations. If you get more people than can fit in a room, split into two rooms for discussion. If more than one discussion group is engaged, at the end of a weekly session, gather the whole group for prayer and sharing something they appreciated about the meeting.

While a kick-off meeting might be skipped by an established or experienced small group, any group will experience awakening and renewal by focusing on the purposes of an outwardly focused community group.

Leading or Hosting a Discussion

- If you are nervous about leading a group discussion, you are a healthy and humble person. God usually speaks through reluctant and ordinary persons. God is already present, working ahead in each life through the means of grace (such as personal prayer or searching the scriptures).

- You have gifts that no one else has in the group. So be yourself and listen. Try to limit your talking time to 20 percent of the discussion so that other participants do 80 percent of the talking.

- You are not alone. Other leaders or good friends can pray for you and prepare with you before the discussion.

- Be ready. Go through the session several times. Listen to the teaching segment for the session on the DVD. Write notes in a Bible or in a journal to listen for what God would speak through you. Don't procrastinate. Prepare before the meeting.

- Get evaluation from the participants. Ask them to send an e-mail or write on cards at the meeting about two or three things they liked from the discussion and one thing that could be improved. Be humble and open to growing as a leader or host.

- Tell your group how this study or group relationships are helping you, personally, draw closer to God and friends. Share your struggles and blessings. Others will see your example and can relate with their own lives.

- Carefully consider another person whom you will ask to lead the group discussion next week. Ask in person, without putting someone on the spot. This is one of the benefits of a community group. The leaders and participants are the same, not experts, because they can't do life alone either.

10 Host Tips

1. Relax! Now, breathe! You can do this, and we're here to help if you get stuck. Remember, God is with you. Pray up, prepare, and be friendly. You can do this! Read Hebrews 13:5.

2. Invite. Now invite some more people to join you for this short six-week journey. You are the key to filling your group. #foundpeoplefindpeople

3. Serve a few snacks. Food helps break the ice. Keep it simple and then share this responsibility weekly with your group members.

4. Prepare for your time together. Preview the DVD, write down your thoughts, and select questions that you feel will work best in your group. #growingpeoplechange

5. Pray for your group members. Follow up with them during the week about the concerns in their lives. Make prayer and reaching out to God a regular part of group life. #worshipisalifestyle

6. Maintain a healthy atmosphere. Don't allow anyone, including yourself, to dominate discussion or fall into gossip. Redirect gently when conversation deviates.

7. Be prepared for questions. As questions arise, don't feel like you have to know all the answers. Just say, "I don't know. Let me check that out." Then contact the church office for some help.

8. Allow silence. When you ask questions, if there is silence for a moment, don't jump in too quickly to rescue. This may just be a sign that people are thoughtful about how to respond.

9. Tackle a mission project together! How can you and your group make a difference in the world? Do it! We'd love to hear your stories about it and see pictures! #savedpeopleservepeople

10. Have fun! Plan to do something in this six-week time outside of the group time together just for fun. It helps build friendships and makes the journey more fun together! #youcan'tdolifealone

Community Group Roster

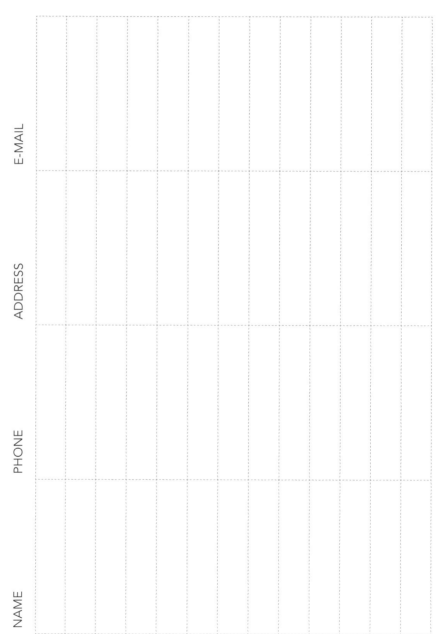

NAME PHONE ADDRESS E-MAIL

Notes

Notes

Notes

Notes

DON'T STOP NOW!

Keep digging into God's word. These studies are
available from Jim and Jennifer Cowart,
published by Abingdon Press.

Living the Five:
Participant and Leader Book

ISBN: 978-1-5018-2509-5

Living the Five: DVD

ISBN: 978-1-5018-2511-8

Grab, Gather, Grow:
Multiply Community Groups in Your Church

ISBN: 978-1-5018-2505-7

Grab, Gather, Grow: DVD

ISBN: 978-1-5018-2508-8

ALSO AVAILABLE

Hand Me Downs
Participant and Leader Book
ISBN: 978-1-5018-2517-0
Hand Me Downs: DVD
ISBN: 978-1-5018-2519-4